The Little
GERMAN ABC
Coloring Book

Nina Barbaresi

DOVER PUBLICATIONS, INC.
New York

Published in Canada by General Publishing Company, Ltd., 30 Lesmill Road, Don Mills, Toronto, Ontario.

Published in the United Kingdom by Constable and Company, Ltd., 3 The Lanchesters, 162–164 Fulham Palace Road, London W6 9ER.

The Little German ABC Coloring Book is a new work, first published by Dover Publications, Inc., in 1993.

International Standard Book Number: 0-486-27463-2

Manufactured in the United States of America
Dover Publications, Inc., 31 East 2nd Street, Mineola, N.Y. 11501

The Little
GERMAN ABC
Coloring Book

Apfel

Buch

Cherub

Dachshund

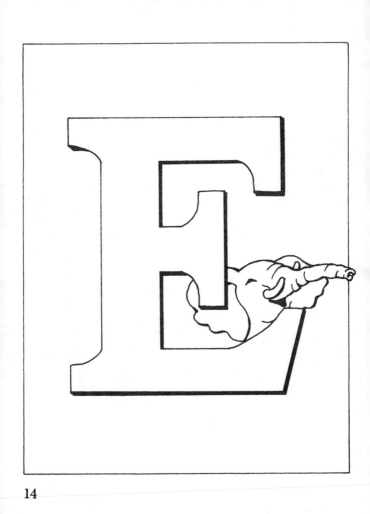

Elefant

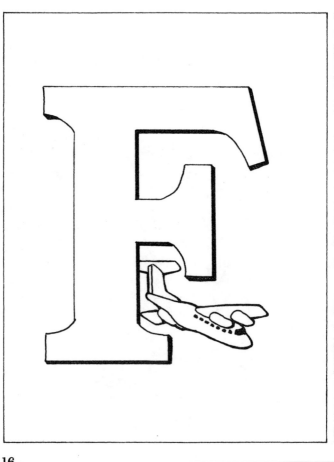

Flugzeug

Giraffe

Hexe

Insel

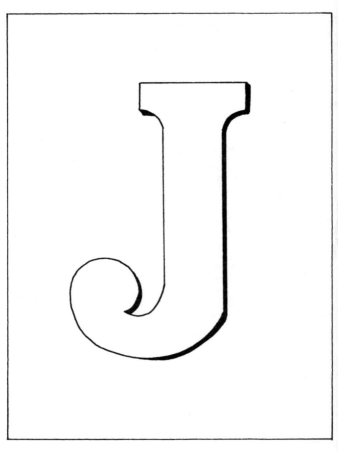

24

Jacke

Katze

Löwe

Mann

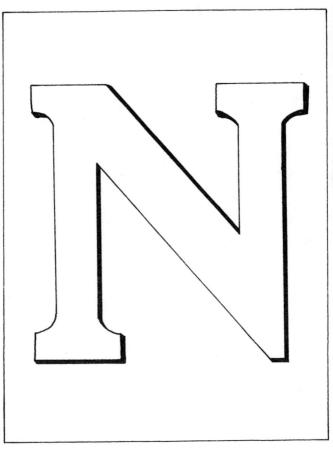

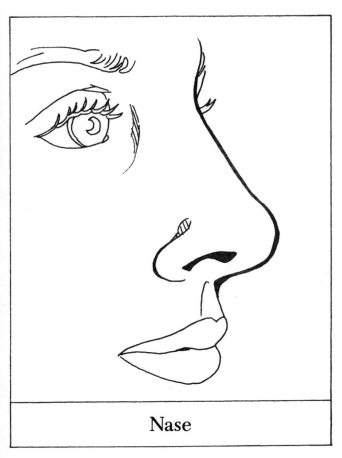

Nase

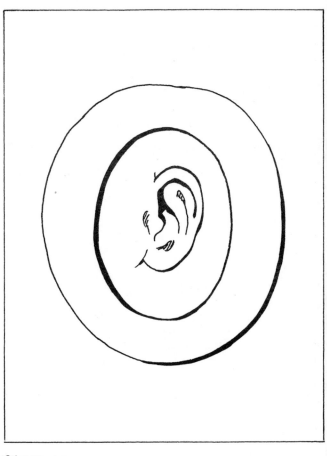

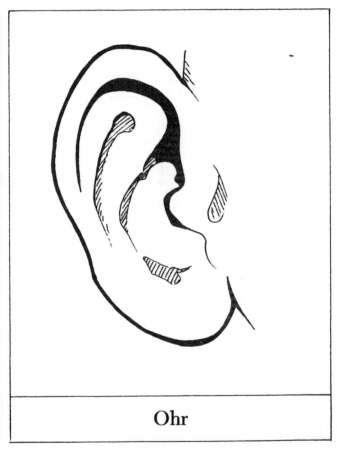

Ohr

Pfau

Qualle

Renntier

Schiff

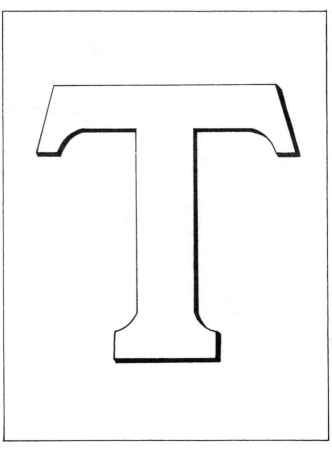

Tisch

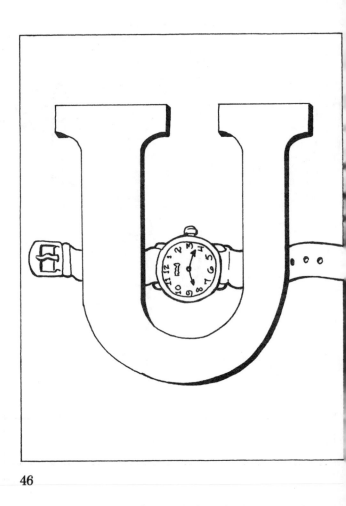

Uhr

Vogel

Wolf

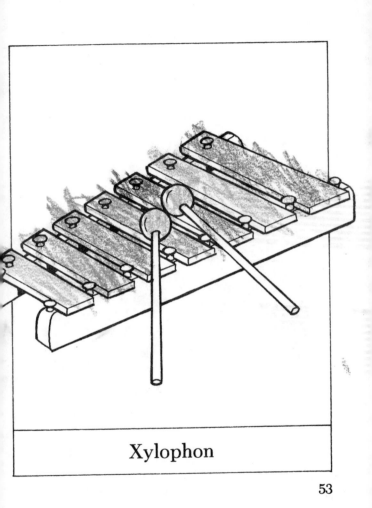

Xylophon

Yo-Yospiel

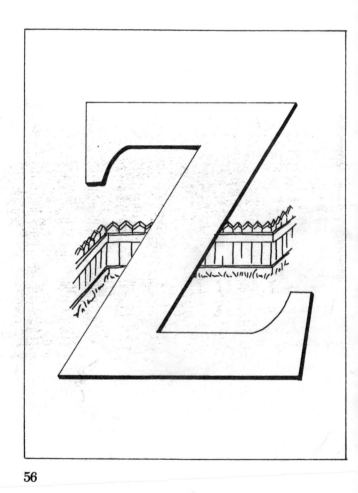

Zaun

Note

Whether children are studying German as a first or as a second language, they need to begin by learning the alphabet and acquiring useful vocabulary. One of the most enjoyable and effective ways to help them remember the letters and new words is by activity, especially in the form of coloring. The present book contains a full German alphabet keyed to essential everyday words, to the names of animals and familiar objects, all charmingly illustrated. To help children "think in German," only the German words for the items illustrated appear in the main part of the book. On pages 61–62, the full word list is repeated, not only with English equivalents (forming a handy glossary) but also with the gender-indicating definite articles, which ideally should be learned along with the words.

German-English Word List

der Apfel	the apple
das Buch	the book
der Cherub	the cherub
der Dachshund	the dachshund
der Elefant	the elephant
das Flugzeug	the airplane
die Giraffe	the giraffe
die Hexe	the witch
die Insel	the island
die Jacke	the jacket
die Katze	the cat
der Löwe	the lion
der Mann	the man

die Nase	the nose
das Ohr	the ear
der Pfau	the peacock
die Qualle	the jellyfish
das Renntier	the reindeer
das Schiff	the ship
der Tisch	the table
die Uhr	the watch, the clock
der Vogel	the bird
der Wolf	the wolf
das Xylophon	the xylophone
das Yo-Yospiel	the yo-yo
der Zaun	the fence